BRANCH LINE TO WANTAGE

WANTAGE

THE WANTAGE TRAMWAY

A Tramway Classic

Vic Mitchell and Keith Smith

MP Middleton Press

Cover picture: No. 5 was built by George England in 1857 and car 4 had been constructed as a double deck electric tram in 1900. The bizarre combination stands near a main line wagon and close to a dilapidated engine shed at Wantage. (J.K.Williams coll.)

Published 2003

ISBN 1 904474 25 X

© Middleton Press, 2003

Design   Deborah Esher
            David Pede
Typesetting   Barbara Mitchell

Published by
            Middleton Press
            Easebourne Lane
            Midhurst, West Sussex
            GU29 9AZ
Tel: 01730 813169
Fax: 01730 812601
Email: info@middletonpress.co.uk
www.middletonpress.co.uk

Printed & bound by MPG Books, Bodmin, Cornwall

CONTENTS

ACKNOWLEDGEMENTS

We are very grateful for the assistance received from many of those mentioned in the credits also to W.R.Burton, M.Butson, G.Croughton, A.Finch, Dr R.J.Harley, J.B.Horne, P.J.Kelley, N.Langridge, Mr D. and Dr S.Salter, G.T.V.Stacey and especially our always supportive wives Barbara Mitchell and Janet Smith; and we are particularly appreciative of the help given by J.Meatcher and his *Guide to References and Sources to the Wantage Tramway*.

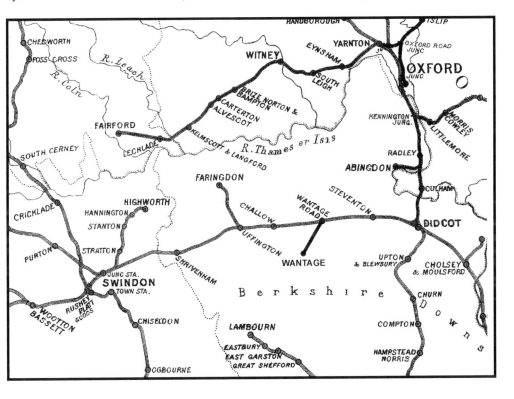

Based on the Railway Clearing House map.

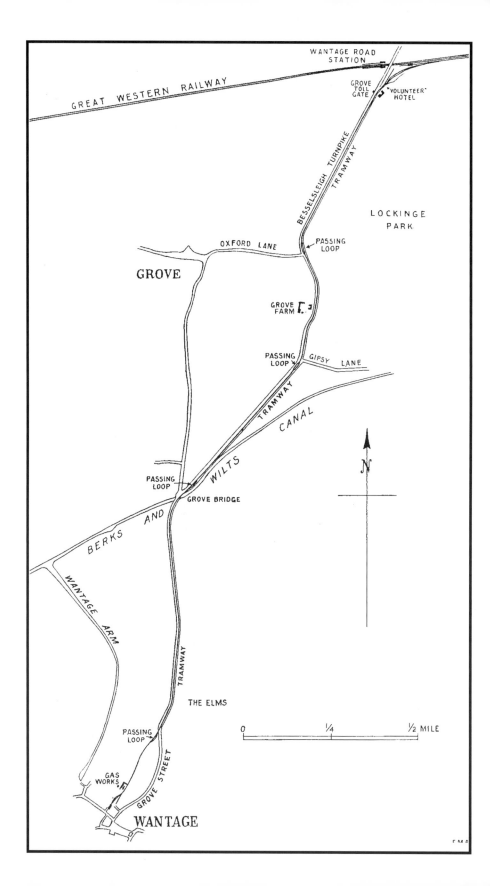

GEOGRAPHICAL SETTING

The old established market town of Wantage is situated at the foot of the steep scarp slope of the Chalk of Lambourn Downs, near the spring line. Below the Chalk is a bed of Upper Greensand and under this is a layer of Gault Clay. Both outcrop north of the town and thus the line traverses them on its 2½ mile route towards the Vale of the White Horse.

The maps are to the scale of 25 inches to 1 mile with north at the top, unless otherwise indicated.

HISTORICAL BACKGROUND

The Great Western Railway opened its route through Wantage Road on 17th December 1840, Wantage being one of several small towns to be left remote from the main line. Initially broad gauge, this part of the London to Bristol route could accommodate standard gauge trains from 1872.

The Tramways Act of 1870 encouraged rail transport extension and thus the Wantage Tramway Co Ltd was incorporated on 10th November 1873 to provide a horse-worked roadside line. Construction began in August 1874 and passenger conveyance started on 11th October 1875. Freight traffic had begun ten days earlier.

Authority to use mechanical propulsion was given on 26th June 1876 and a steam tram began operation on 1st August of that year (see pictures nos 3 and 4: the following illustrations show subsequent developments using small locomotives).

Moderate prosperity ensued and the investors derived a satisfactory return for most years, up to and including the final one. However, developments in road vehicles resulted in the GWR starting a competing bus service in 1924. The end of tramway passenger services followed on 1st August 1925, but goods traffic continued until 22nd December 1945.

1.   The diagram shows the four passing loops that existed in 1877. The number was halved in the light of experience and they were eventually turned into sidings in which passenger services waited while goods trains passed by. Oxford Lane and Grove Bridge remained to the end.
(F.Merton Atkins)

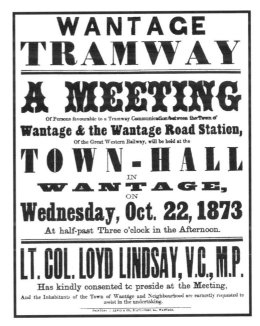

2.   The poster for the inaugural meeting did not reveal that the enterprising promoters were intent on using mechanical means of propulsion at the earliest opportunity. However, it was to be 1876 before Royal Assent was given to the company for such action to be taken. The tramway was later recorded as the first in Britain to use such power. (M.J.Stretton coll.)

PASSENGER SERVICES

The journeys were timed to make connections with GWR up and down departures. There were corresponding connections with arrivals, the same tram simply waiting a short while. The GWR provided a slip coach from London at 10.30am in 1884, but, as few used it, a connecting tram was provided on Wednesdays only, after an initial trial period.

Departures from Wantage in sample years are listed right. They are weekdays only; no Sunday cars were operated.

1879	1905	1923
am	am	am
7.05	7.05	7.08
9.25	7.40	8.10
pm	9.15	9.30
12.08	9.35	9.48
12.40	11.00	10.25
2.17	pm	pm
5.25	12.05	12.10
6.05	1.25	2.20
8.20	2.25	3.15
	3.10	5.40
	5.35	6.32
	6.15	7.35
	6.30	8.18
	7.50	
	8.30	

3.   The tram was included as one of the five notable items in the district in late Victorian times. (Postcard)

MOTIVE POWER

4.   Mr John Grantham filed a patent in 1871 for a steam propelled tramcar and the prototype was completed in 1873. The flue from the central boiler divided the longitudinal seat on the upper deck. The boiler and mechanism were built by Merryweather & Sons, a firm noted for its fine fire engines. A means of indicating and *recording* its speed was provided. (J.K.Williams coll.)

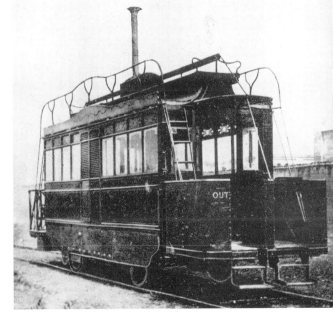

5.   The car had its first trial in London, on the route to Victoria during the night of 23rd November 1873, but it was to be almost a year before it was inspected by representatives of the Wantage Tramway. It was eventually hired and given a test on 18th September 1875. It went into regular service on 1st August 1876 and was recorded as operating the first steam tram service in Britain.The Grantham car was purchased in September 1876 and seems to have worked until October 1887, after which time it was locomotive hauled. It was sold in 1891 and has been incorrectly recorded in a history of steam trams as having gone to Cowplain. (J.K.Williams coll.)

6.   No. 4, the Hughes tram engine, was intended mainly for goods traffic and was thus fitted with buffers, but the coupling was unorthodox. It arrived on 24th March 1877 and was probably the second such machine to be built by the firm. It had a condenser which could be used to reduce the amount of steam issued when running near the road. It usually ran without coupling rods and was sold in 1919. (J.K.Williams coll.)

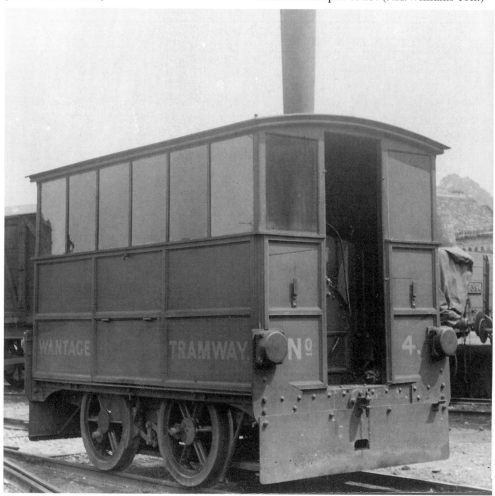

7.   No. 6 was Matthews Patent Tramway Engine, which was built at F.W.Jackson's Kingsbury Ironworks and completed in 1881. It also had a condenser, but was fitted with full skirting to comply with tramway legislation concerning exposed moving parts. The photo is from 2nd April 1923. (J.K.Williams coll.)

8.   The skirt panels were hinged at the top and the nearest one (with the bulge) covered the cylinder. The engine arrived on trial in January 1882 and was deemed unsatisfactory. However, it was eventually purchased (in 1888) and ran until 1925. It was photographed in September 1920 and cut up in 1931. (K.Nunn/LCGB)

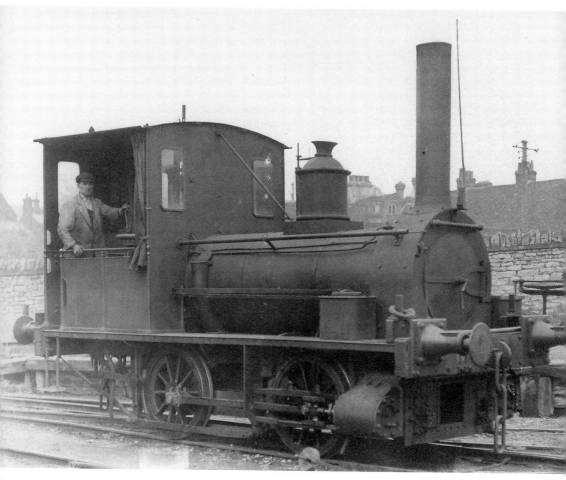

9.   No. 5 was the first conventional engine purchased by the tramway, although it did not have a condenser or skirting. It was built by George England at New Cross in 1857 and was recorded in May 1930. This firm also provided the first locomotives for the Festiniog Railway and the 1863 *Prince* is still operational. (H.C.Casserley)

10. No. 5 worked in Crewe Works for almost 15 years until the LNWR sold it to the tramway in May 1878 for handling the goods traffic. This low angle view from 1924 shows the pole under the buffer beam for coupling to the tramcars. (K.Nunn/LCGB)

11. No. 5 had a new boiler fitted by the GWR at Swindon in 1896 and further major overhauls in 1921 and 1939. It is thus strange that it did not receive this plate until 1941. (F.A.Wycherley)

12. With commendable foresight, the GWR purchased no. 5 at the clearance sale in 1946, acquiring the historic treasure for £100. It is seen after cosmetic restoration in Swindon Works on 4th July 1947, with *North Star* and *Carmarthen Castle* in the background. (H.C.Casserley)

13. No. 5 was put on display under a new shelter at Wantage Road station in April 1948. She was fitted with her original name of *Shannon*, although she was always known as *Jane* on the tramway. (J.K.Williams coll.)

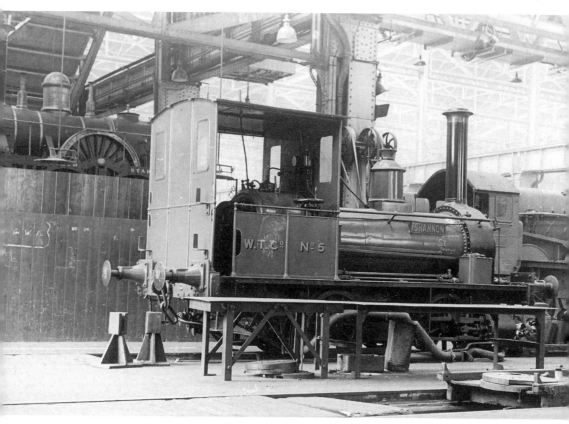

14. The number 7 was given to this Manning Wardle 0-4-0ST, which was purchased from the Manchester Ship Canal in 1893 for which it had been built in 1888. (J.K.Williams coll.)

15. The manufacturer's standard minimal cab was extended extensively by the time it was photographed at Swindon in 1927. This works had fitted a new boiler in 1900, this being reported as "rebuilt" in 1921. (RAS Marketing)

16. No. 7 was considered to be the line's most successful locomotive and was not withdrawn until 1945. It is seen on 10th May 1930 at Wantage. The name *Mary* was often used, but never applied. (H.C.Casserley)

17. No. 7 avoided the cutting torch in 1946 as she was purchased by A.R.Adams & Son of Newport (Mon). She was photographed at Newport on 12th July 1958 during an obviously emotional visit by admirers, two of whom bow their heads and one holds his stomach. This was an RCTS visit. (R.M.Casserley)

18.   This and the next picture feature no. 7 on 30th September 1961, while at Cordes Steel Mills at Newport. Devoid of a coupling chain and with battered chimney and cab, she was still carrying a lamp. (J.K.Williams coll.)

E 10. WANTAGE TRAMWAY.

WANTAGE
TO
Wantage   Road.
SECOND 6d SINGLE.

19.   Although once a common contractors locomotive, few Manning Wardles survived into the 1960s. No. 7 was broken up by E.L.Pitt & Co. (Coventry) Ltd on site in December 1963. The wheelbase was only 4ft 9ins. The WT bought another Manning Wardle in 1919, but it was a failure and soon scrapped. Named *The Driver*, it came from Woolwich Arsenal. (J.K.Williams coll.)

20.   No. 1329 was purchased from the GWR in March 1910 and its number was retained by the tramway throughout the remainder of its life. This came in 1920, when it was scrapped; it had been withdrawn in 1910. (J.K.Williams coll.)

I 4.   WANTAGE   TRAMWAY.

WANTAGE ROAD
TO
Grove Bridge.
SECOND 4½d. SINGLE.

21.   An earlier view of no. 1329 shows its previous GWR number and also the name once carried. It had been built for the broad gauge South Devon Railway by the Avonside Engine Co. in 1874. The GWR converted it to standard gauge in 1892 and changed its number at that time. (J.K.Williams coll.)

I 42.   WANTAGE   TRAMWAY.

WANTAGE ROAD
TO
Grove Bridge.

SECOND 4½d. SINGLE.

22.   A splendid panorama from about 1892 features the Hughes tram engine with car nos 1, 2 and 3 in correct numerical order. Nos 1 and 2 were initially horse drawn and were provided by the Starbuck Car & Wagon Company of Birkenhead in 1875. No. 1 had a portable ladder, but it seems the top deck was seldom used. (S.P.Higgins coll./NRM)

23.   Car 3 was supplied by G.F.Milnes (successor to Starbuck) in 1890 and it ran to the end of passenger services. No. 4, in the original numbering, was similar to car 5, seen in the next picture. (P.Q.Treloar coll.)

24.   This is one of two cars bought from the Reading Tramway Co. Ltd on 30th July 1903, when it abandoned horse traction. The top deck seating was removed and both were sold in 1912. (Brunel University/Clinker coll.)

25.   The second no. 4 and no. 5 came new from Hurst, Nelson & Co. Ltd in 1912. This is no. 4, which had been fitted with a top deck for an exhibition in 1900 and was probably a bargain after prolonged storage and removal of electrical equipment. (B.S.Jennings coll.)

26.   No. 5 was set aside near car 4 at Wantage and still had all its windows intact when photographed in September 1930. It was part of an order for Bradford Corporation, which had been cancelled. (Milepost 92½ coll.)

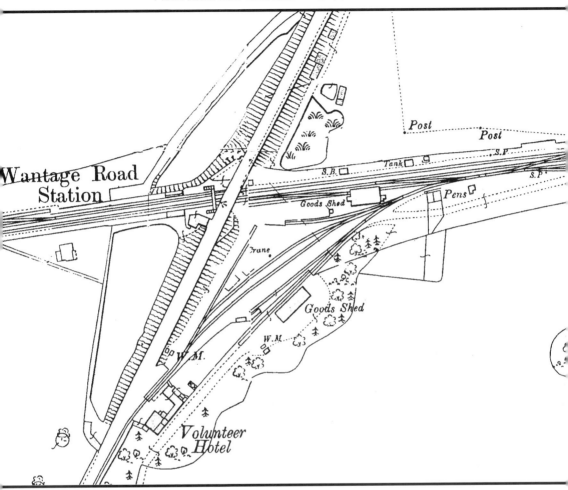

27.   The 1912 survey has the tramway from Wantage at the lower border. Passenger cars used the short siding parallel to the main road. The lower goods shed and siding were the property of the Lockinge Estate.

28. This 1919 view towards London includes the brick arched road bridge beyond the steel footbridge. The wide space between the tracks is a legacy from the days of the broad gauge. (LGRP/NRM)

──────────▶

29. A closer view of the goods shed in 1932 includes work in progress on the quadrupling of the tracks. In the background is the new signal box; a new water tank was built on the left. (British Railways)

──────────▶

30. The new steel spans for the road bridge used part of the old southern abutment and passengers continued to pass under the road, on the right, instead of going through the building. (British Railways)

31.   A view of the other side of the bridge includes the pathway under the road, once used by tram passengers. The trams had earlier stood on the extreme left. (British Railways)

——————→

32.   The approach to the station was recorded in about the 1930s. The GWR required the tramway to be fenced on its entry to the goods yard; all traffic ceased in it on 29th March 1965. The landlord of "The Volunteer" and his wife were given free travel on the trams in 1891. (LGRP)

——————→

33.   We complete our survey of the station by looking west from the road bridge soon after the quadrupling westwards was completed in 1933. A wagon stands in the up siding, beyond the new platform. (Brunel University/Mowat coll.)

I 49. WANTAGE TRAMWAY.
———
WANTAGE ROAD
TO
Grove Bridge.
SECOND IJI. SINGLE.

34.   Seen not long before closure to passengers on 7th December 1964, the station was by that time little used. Most of the soot is to be seen above the main lines. (Lens of Sutton)

35.   Although not visible in the previous picture the shelter on the down platform and no. 5
Shannon remained until November 1966. She was stored nearby and taken to Didcot in 1969.
(J.K.Williams coll.)

Other views of this station appear in our
Didcot to Swindon *album.*

36.   Cars 3 and 1 are seen at the end of the passenger line, together with the Hughes tram engine. Goods items were often conveyed on the platforms, as seen. (J.K.Williams coll.)

37.   The sleeper stop at the end of the track is evident again as car 3 is loaded with boxes while no. 4 smokes lazily. The other end of the inclined path is seen in picture 31.
    (J.K.Williams coll.)

38.   The same combination is seen from the other side with no. 4 revealing its coupling pole. Also in view is the GWR's 12-ton crane. The single fare to the town in 1875 was 9d first class and 6d second class. (S.P.Higgins coll./NRM)

G 17.   WANTAGE   TRAMWAY
WANTAGE ROAD
TO
Oxford Lane.
SECOND 3d. SINGLE.

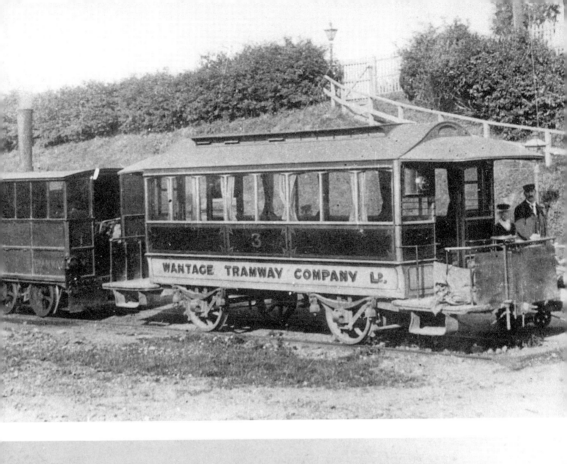

39.   Matthews Patent Tramway Engine waits while items are loaded into bogie car no. 4. The coupling pole is tucked up neatly in this instance. The number of passengers conveyed rose steadily from 36,692 in 1895 to 56,180 in 1906. (S.P.Higgins coll./NRM)

40.   Our final view of a passenger service at this location includes part of the run-round loop that was in place from 1912 to 1928. No. 7 was recorded on 11th September 1920, along with cars 3 and 5. (K.Nunn/LCGB)

41.   The diminutive no. 7 was photographed at work in the yard on 21st June 1939. Occasionally WT engines ran onto the main line to collect or add a van or horsebox. (H.C.Casserley)

42.   No. 7 appears to have an exceptionally long train earlier the same month. However, Mr Casserley was experienced at persuading crews to move stock to give the best impression. He did the same with his fashionable Austin 10. (H.C.Casserley)

THE JOURNEY

43.   The station building is in the distance as no. 4 waits to be photographed with cars 1 and 3. The driver has his hand on the regulator, which is above the smokebox door. (J.K.Williams coll.)

44.   No. 7 was recorded near the start of its journey to Wantage on 11th September 1920, hauling three cars; this may have been the "school run". The GWR took over the WT's parcel service on 1st August 1925. (K.Nunn/LCGB)

45.   No. 7 and the Austin 10 appear again on 17th June 1939, but with the train shorter than seen in picture 42. A telephone link between the termini had been provided in about 1905. (H.C.Casserley)

46.   Exhibiting one shiny bald tyre, an Austin Six was used for a posed press photograph on 2nd January 1936. The report named no. 5 as *Jane*, presumably the wife of one of the drivers. She never carried a nameplate on the WT. (Hulton Archive/Getty Images)

47.   A rather less professional photo features no. 7 with the usual assortment of wagons for Wantage. The boxes above the cylinders contain sand, often a necessity on such grass infested track. (Lens of Sutton)

48.   No. 5 is seen on part of the track where the highway came up to the outer rail. Originally the tramway was in the road, but at one side of it, with "tarmacadam extending eighteen inches beyond each rail". The stovepipe was short lived. (Lens of Sutton)

49.   Highway improvements eventually meant that the tramway no longer provided a better surface than the local authority. For many years, three goods trips were run each day, but the traffic was sometimes imbalanced, as was the case for no. 7 on 11th September 1920. The first trip up in the morning was often as "light engine". (K.Nunn/LCGB)

50.   No. 5 was photographed in perfect light conditions on the day before cessation of passenger services. It is at the Oxford Lane stop; the siding is in the grass on the left. (F.E.J.Burgiss coll.)

51.   No. 7 runs north near Gypsy Lane on 30th July 1938 with two empty Ecklington coal wagons. The telephone wires had to be well spaced as they were uninsulated. (V.R.Webster/Kidderminster Railway Museum)

52.   Canal Cottages are in the background
as no. 7 proceeds while attached to a ten-ton
van endorsed FLOUR TRAFFIC ONLY Empty
to WANTAGE ROAD in 1939. This was an
important traffic on the WT, the mill being close
to Lower Yard. (H.C.Casserley)

53.   Running near Grove Bridge in about
1905 is no. 4, which is hauling cars 3, 1 and 4,
the latter being ex-Reading. The maximum
speed was set at 10mph.
(S.P.Higgins coll./NRM)

54.   Car 3 is featured in the same vicinity, along with Hughes tram engine no. 4 and car 1.
Grove Bridge was another stopping point. One rail of the siding is visible on the left and the
bridge is in the background. (J.K.Williams coll.)

55. A lady is assisted from car 3 and no wonder it was necessary when one assesses the height of the step from the ground. First and second class had been abolished on the first day of 1889. (Reading Library)

56. The driver is wearing a cap, but in Summer the Matthews patent must have been like a mobile heated glasshouse. However, car 5, and the others, would have been like ice houses in mid-Winter. (J.K.Williams coll.)

57. No. 7 with car 4 appeared in another postcard view of this popular tramway. The WT took a lease on the turnpike road and thus took tolls from other road users, but exempted itself. The toll ceased in November 1878. (J.K.Williams coll.)

58.   No. 5 was photographed working the mid-day goods to Wantage Mill Street on 10th May 1930, while the cyclist at its rear was recorded as being the goods clerk returning from Wantage Road. (H.C.Casserley)

59.   The road drops away from track level in this fine picture of no. 7 with car 4 in about 1914. The tramway and the road passed over the canal on separate bridges. (Lens of Sutton)

60.   A photograph from 19th July 1946 shows no. 7 involved with track dismantling. For many years there had been three trips down to Wantage Road, usually at 8am and 11am and 4pm. (J.K.Williams coll.)

61.   At about noon on 8th January 1936, no. 5 left the road while hauling five loaded coal wagons to Wantage. Four remained on the track, which was deemed to be the cause of the trouble. The staff laboured through the night and had all traffic running by 11.0am the next day. The site was about 150yds south of the canal bridge. (Hulton Archive/Getty Images)

62.   No. 5 had a similar problem back in February 1921. A pair of re-railing ramps was eventually purchased in 1925. No. 5 usually took up to five wagons to Wantage and 12 to 14 down to the GWR. (J.Meatcher coll.)

63.   No. 7 struggles towards Wantage with a leaking gland on 17th June 1939, displaying a pair of lamps. There was a rare case of a foreign train running on the line in 1909. It was composed of SECR four-wheeled stock and was provided for a military funeral. (H.C.Casserley)

64.　Nearing the end of its journey from Wantage Road on 11th April 1944 is Manning Wardle no. 7. The van often contained some of the output of Clark & Sons' Town Mills. For many years, they despatched over 600 tons of flour per month. (F.A.Wycherley)

65.　After crossing the road, the line to Lower Yard diverged right. This opened on 1st July 1905 and greatly relieved congestion at Upper Yard in Mill Street. (LGRP)

66.　Wartime posters are exhibited as no. 5 takes to the company's own track and issues steam from inappropriate parts. The line climbed at 1 in 47 from here towards Upper Yard, but this section was known as the "The Cutting". (S.P.Higgins/NRM)

L 10　WANTAGE　TRAMWAY.

WANTAGE ROAD
TO
Grove Bridge.
FIRST **10d.** RETURN.

67.   A photograph from 2nd January 1936 reveals that, even on Grove Street crossing, grooved tramway rail was not used. The line had been laid with bridge rails at 40lbs/ft, but was later relaid with flat bottom material, much of it 56lbs/ft. The street lamp had once had one red glass to indicate danger. (Hulton Archive/Getty Images)

68.   No. 5 was positioned for photography on 9th April 1936 alongside the ground once occupied by a passing loop. This was reduced to a short siding later. The Standard Swallow was first registered in 1932. (J.H.L.Adams, Kidderminster Railway Museum)

69.   A future railway photographer was in training as no. 7 was posed for posterity at the same location, but on the points, on 17th June 1939. War was imminent and such pleasures could never be repeated again. (H.C.Casserley)

70.   No. 7 is seen on the same day approaching one of the two massive warning signs. Presumably the standard cast iron signs could not be used on a tramway legally. (H.C.Casserley)

WANTAGE -
PASSENGER ERA

71.   The map from 1877 has the initial simple arrangement, as shown in the next illustration. The canal wharf is on the left; the Wantage Arm is shown on map 1. The Wantage Gas & Coke Company had been formed in 1840.

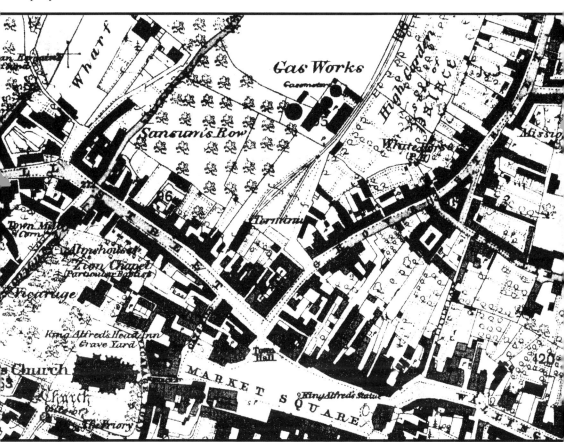

72.   One of the earliest photographs of the terminus appropriately features no. 5 and is thought to date from about 1892. Until the advent of the tramway, most coal for the town had come by canal, mainly from Somerset and Gloucestershire pits. (S.P.Higgins coll./NRM)

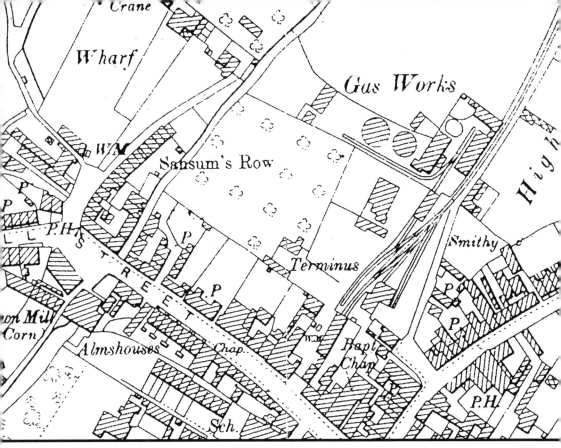

73.   The 1896 survey includes the track extension into the gasworks and a siding beside the gas holders. The canal basin is to the left of the crane. The gas company had been purchased by the Wantage Urban Sanitary Authority in 1879 and was transferred to the Wantage Urban District Council in 1934.

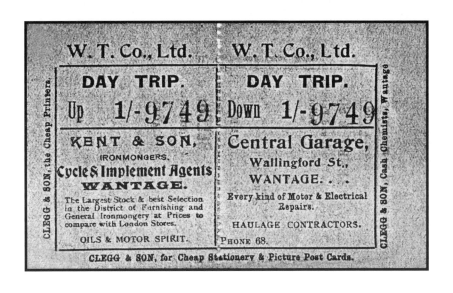

74.   Two for the price of one as nos 5 and 7 stand by a point lever, sometime before 1914. The fine fretwork on car 5 is shown to advantage. Fares were always high on the WT; for example, 6d single in 1889 and 9d in 1923, when the driver earned £3 a week. (J.K.Williams coll.)

75.   An early postcard included mention of trials of a compressed air tram engine in 1880. It worked well, but fuel cost was about five times higher. No. 6 is featured with car 3.
(Lens of Sutton)

76.   A closer look at no. 6 in work-weary condition shows a toe hole, used in place of a projecting step. The view includes the coal stage and ash heaps. (K.Nunn/LCGB)

77.   No. 6 blows off as the crew looks directly at the camera, the windows being too dirty for use. The passenger is on a bench above the battered end panel of car 3. (F.E.J.Burgiss coll.)

78.   Our first picture of Lower Yard was probably a promotional one taken soon after its opening in 1905. Vans stand on the sidings in the background. The Anglo-American Oil Company took a lease on part of the yard in 1924 and laid out oil tanks. (J.Meatcher coll.)

G 11   WANTAGE   TRAMWAY.

WANTAGE ROAD
TO
Oxford Lane.
SECOND 3d. SINGLE.

79.   The panel is further dented in this picture from 1923. The cause of the damage was probably the buffers of wagons or locomotives. No. 7 has its coupling pole in use and the guard is wearing his cash satchel.
(A.W.Croughton/M.J.Stretton)

80.   Steam partially obscures the crane as no. 5 rests between duties on 26th April 1924. Back in 1904, 3603 wagons were conveyed from the GWR, this increasing to 5707 by 1911. (K.Nunn/LCGB)

81.   Seen on the same day, no. 5 has its coupling pole resting in a hook; this should be a sure way of dating photos as prior to 1925. Not so, as most remained in place long after the cars retired. (K.Nunn/LCGB)

82.   Tram loco no. 6 is unusually sandwiched between cars 3 and 6, not long before withdrawal of the passenger service. The company's office is on the right, the 1876 building including a waiting room. (F.E.J.Burgiss coll.)

83.   A view across the yard includes a horse waiting for coal and the remainder of the crane jib. The crane came from the canal wharf in about 1905. Cars 6 and 3 stand amongst the horse droppings, a feature of most stations of this period. (Lens of Sutton)

84.   Unfortunately the occasion of this staff photograph with no. 7 and car 3 was no recorded. During the early 1920s the payrol included a chief fitter, an assistant, a managing clerk, three engine drivers, a conductor, a porter a checker and a carter. (F.E.J.Burgiss coll.)

85.   The tram shed has appeared in several views, but this is the first to reveal that the platform was against the wall. Car 3 stands as spare, which explains the apparent sandwiching in picture 82. (J.K.Williams coll.)

86.   After crossing the back of the previous picture, passengers would emerge into Mill Street through the gateway on the left of this view. The adjacent building carries the words WANTAGE TRAMWAY Co. Ltd. 1904, a sign of some opulence at that time. (Postcard)

C 9   WANTAGE   TRAMWAY.

WANTAGE

TO

Oxford Lane.

SECOND 4½d. SINGLE.

WANTAGE -
GOODS ONLY ERA

87.   The decaying goods platform is evident in this fine view of no. 7 on 10th May 1930. The
tramway had suffered a major loss of revenue when Town Mills traffic ceased in 1917. However,
it returned later. The head lights were obtained in 1904. (H.C.Casserley)

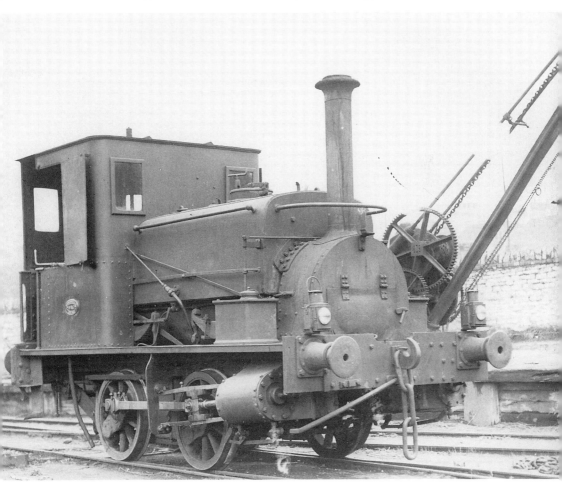

E S.   WANTAGE   TRAMWAY.

WANTAGE
TO
Wantage   Road.
SECOND 6d SINGLE.

88.   The crane was of value when steel plate arrived in special wagons of this type. There were no lights in the yard. On 29th January 1903 the manager was instructed to obtain one gaslight for the platform, 80 boiler tubes and one lavatory. (Lens of Sutton)

K 7   WANTAGE TRAMWAY.

WANTAGE ROAD
TO
Grove Bridge.

SECOND 8d. RETURN.

89.　　Car 5 and tram engine no. 6 were still intact in May 1930. Maybe the directors were dreaming of a passenger revival, although leaded coloured top lights were long out of fashion by that time. (H.C.Casserley)

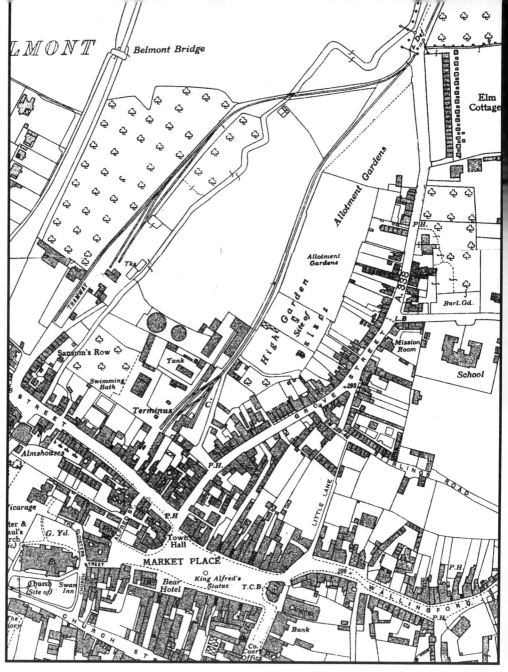

90.   The 1937 map includes the full length of both branches. Lower Yard (left) was linked with Upper Yard by telephone in 1921 and a connection to the national system was made at that time. This had been possible in 1906, but the directors had rejected such modern devices. *Tks* indicates oil storage tanks. Gas production ceased on 17th March 1947, but the holders remained in use until March 1958.

Gas Coal Conveyed (tons)

1900	1010	1938	2270
1914	1650	1941	2562
1931	2024	1945	2974

91.　　Nos 5 and 7 stand outside the locomotive shed, sometime in the 1930s. It had been necessary to have two engines in steam in passenger days. The cars were unlit until 1892. (R.S.Carpenter coll.)

92.　　The short wheelbase of no. 7 would have given the driver a rough ride; he is shunting the yard after the completion of his 2½ mile journey. Note that the coal was supplied in very large lumps. (Lens of Sutton)

93.   The inspection pit appears in this and the previous picture. This also includes a timber drag, abandoned near the crane. A byproduct of gas production was ammoniacal liquor and tar which was conveyed in the gas company's tank wagon to a tar distillery. (R.S.Carpenter coll.)

94.   Sanitary ware is stacked high in the background - the pipes are salt glazed earthenware. The driver is holding the brake handle, which acted on only two blocks - they are behind the rear wheels. (Lens of Sutton)

95.   Another view of no. 7 and this includes the route to the gasworks, through the running shed. During World War II there were two trackmen, a fitter, a driver, a clerk, an assistant, a shunter, a yardman, two lorry drivers and three horse drivers. (LGRP/P.Q.Treloar coll.)

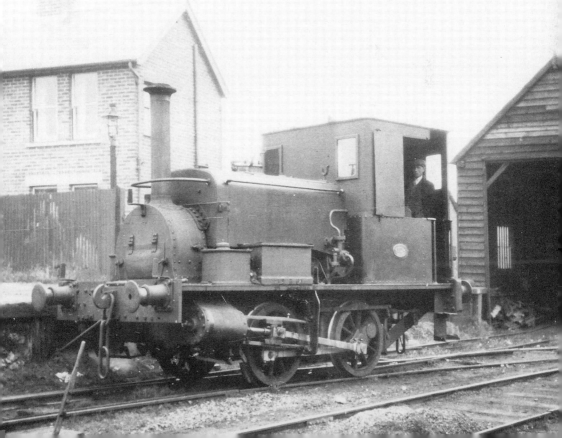

→

96.   A southward panorama of Lower Yard in 1939 includes its squat office, right of centre. The lorry has brought sacks of flour from the mill in the background. Much of this was destined for Reading for biscuit making. (W.A.Camwell)

97.   Lower Yard had a rural location which made an ideal background for a photograph of a graceful old lady, although groaning about the bearings by 1935. No. 5 would have been 78 years old at that time. (F.M.Butterfield/Lens of Sutton)

→

98.   After an evening run back, no. 7 was still displaying a red oil lamp for the benefit of motorists. The purpose of the chain is evident later. Note that the wheels and motion are coated with mud. (S.P.Higgins coll./NRM)

99.   The gable ends are, from left to right, the Baptist Chapel, the workshop, the original shed and the former station, which had been sheeted over to form a garage. (S.P.Higgins coll./NRM)

100.   This photo of no. 7 gives us another glimpse of Lower Yard, the buildings of which were roofed with Belgian-style pantiles, produced in vast quantities in Bridgwater. The initial letters were applied at Swindon in 1939 in the case of no. 5. (Lens of Sutton)

101.   An indifferent view from June 1934 is included to show the appalling state of the track by that time and that steel plate was still being delivered for Wantage Engineering. (Brunel University/Mowat coll.)

102.   Wantage Engineering built eight wagons for the Hampton Waterworks two-foot gauge system in 1914, but its price of £27 each was too high for it to win the order for their main fleet of over 100 coal trucks. In the cramped yard, fly shunting was a necessity. The chain was used to impart some momentum to the wagon and this could often be maintained by the shoulder of the shunter or by a pinch bar under one of its wheels. (Lens of Sutton)

103.   On the left is the engine shed from 1894, which was known as "Small Shed" and through which all coal for the gasworks passed. The WT paid the gasworks one shilling per annum for consent to open the engine shed doors over its land. The photo is from 1939. (Lens of Sutton)

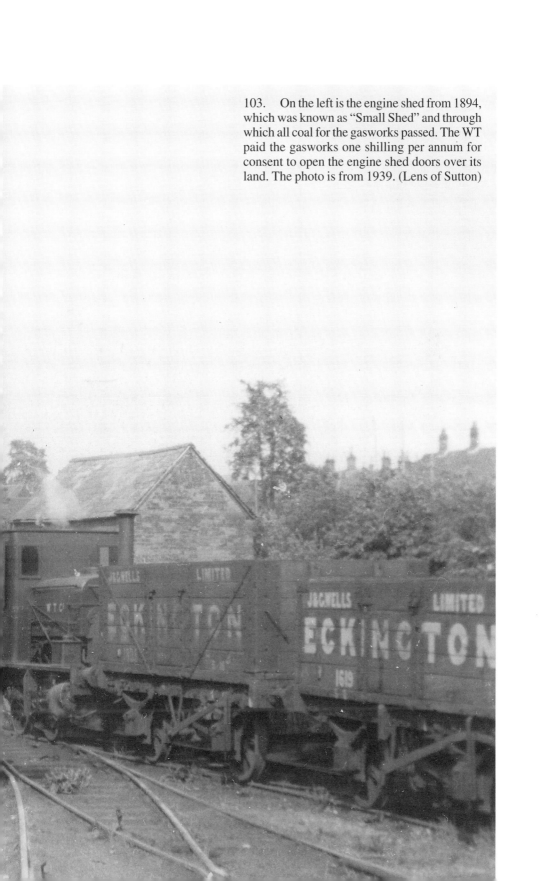

104.   Nos 5 and 7 stand outside Small Shed with parts of the gasworks appearing in the background. One fishplate in the dreadful track has two instead of four bolts. (Lens of Sutton)

105.   This view from the throat shows the short length of the loop and new retort elements for the gasworks. Wantage Engineering sent out by rail mining and ploughing components and brought in steel and coke. (LGRP/P.Q.Treloar)

106.   The WT's horse-drawn timber drags appear again as no. 7 approaches wagons near the crane. Loco mileages survive for September 1922 thus: no. 5-400 and no. 7-105. (Lens of Sutton)

107. The spacious Lower Yard was approached between willows and allotments, and was adjacent to an orchard, a great contrast to the confines of Upper Yard. The boys are admiring no. 5 on 9th April 1936. The sale of fruit produced a revenue of £71 for the WT in 1943. (J.H.L.Adams/Kidderminster Railway Museum)

108. Alongside no. 5 in the weed-infested yard on 17th June 1939 is a stack of new sleepers, no doubt a welcome sight for the drivers. Langford's and Weedon's coal wharf is on the right. (H.C.Casserley)

109. The main line northwards is to the right of no. 7 in this view from 30th July 1938. No. 5 does not appear to be in steam and has her curtain drawn across.
(V.R.Webster/Kidderminster Railway Museum)

110. The shunter leans on the point lever as no. 7 propels one wagon towards the others on the same day. The Oxford Gas Company agreed to purchase the Wantage works in 1944 and to pipe gas to the town. Thus the end of the WT was nigh. (V.R. Webster/Kidderminster Railway Museum)

111. Turning 90° as the train departs north, we see the retort house in the background and can examine Hall's wagon in more detail. This firm did not supply coal to Wantage very regularly. (V.R. Webster/Kidderminster Railway Museum)

112. The first of two final views of operational locomotives shows no. 7 ambling through orchards near Lower Yard on 11th April 1944. Her ashpan damper is revealed for the first time in this volume. (F.A.Wycherley coll.)

113. No. 7 was recorded by the coal stack in Upper Yard on the same day, but probably not in steam. The large diameter sanding pipe is clearly seen. The WT was closed from November 1943 to February 1944 due to the damage to its track caused by the US Army. Thus the company was mortally wounded and went into voluntary liquidation on 29th January 1946. (F.A.Wycherley coll.)

DRAWINGS

114.   No. 5 could seat 22 and was built in 1904 for use on the Nidd Valley Light between Lofthouse and Angram, but it never arrived on that line.

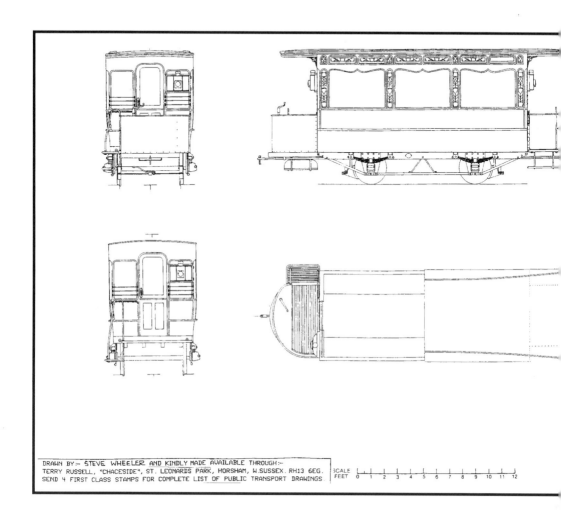

DRAWN BY :- STEVE WHEELER AND KINDLY MADE AVAILABLE THROUGH :-
TERRY RUSSELL, "CHACESIDE", ST. LEONARDS PARK, HORSHAM, W.SUSSEX. RH13 6EG.
SEND 4 FIRST CLASS STAMPS FOR COMPLETE LIST OF PUBLIC TRANSPORT DRAWINGS.

SCALE
FEET 0 1 2 3 4 5 6 7 8 9 10 11 12

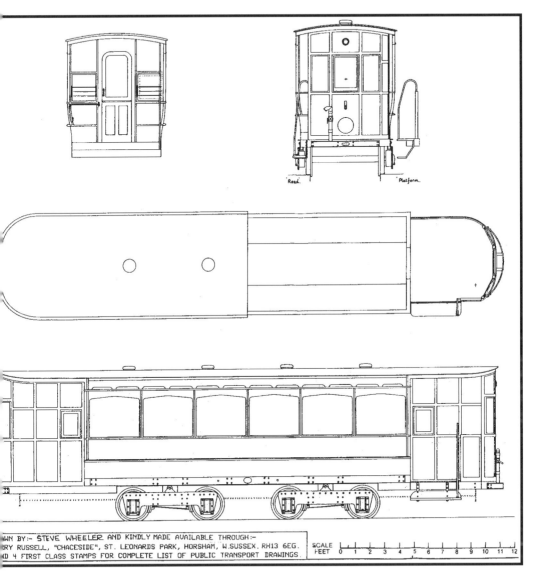

115.   No. 4 was built by Hurst, Nelson & Company of Motherwell, builders of tramcars for systems throughout the United Kingdom. As a double decker it could seat 68.

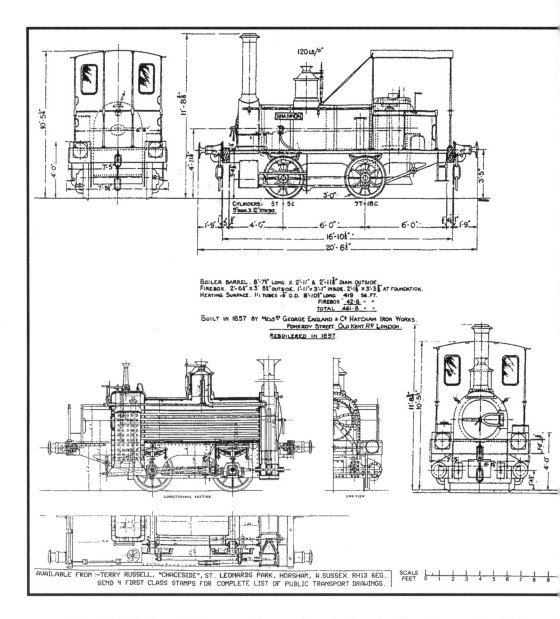

BOILER BARREL. 8'-7¼" LONG. X 2'-11" & 2'-11⅛" DIAM. OUTSIDE.
FIREBOX. 2'-6⅛"X 3' 8⅛"OUTSIDE. 1'-11"X 3'-1" INSIDE. 2'-1⅛"X 3'-3⅝" AT FOUNDATION.
HEATING SURFACE. 111 TUBES 1⅞" O.D. 8'-10¼" LONG   419   SQ. FT.
                                        FIREBOX   42·8   "   "
                                            TOTAL   461·8   "   "
BUILT IN 1857 BY MESS⁵ᴿ GEORGE ENGLAND & C⁰ HATCHAM IRON WORKS.
                    POMEROY STREET. OLD KENT Rᴰ LONDON.
            REBOILERED IN 1897.

LONGITUDINAL SECTION   END VIEW

AVAILABLE FROM :-TERRY RUSSELL, "CHACESIDE", ST. LEONARDS PARK, HORSHAM, W.SUSSEX. RH13 6EG.
SEND 4 FIRST CLASS STAMPS FOR COMPLETE LIST OF PUBLIC TRANSPORT DRAWINGS.

SCALE
FEET   0   1   2   3   4   5   6   7   8   9

116.   No. 5 had carried the name *Shannon* for only about her first six years, it referring to a
former frigate. She was built without a cab for the Sandy & Potton Railway in Bedfordshire,
which became part of the LNWR in 1862. The drawing was produced by the GWR in 1946.

FINALE

117.   A northward view from the passenger platform in 1957 is across the site of the middle of the trackwork. The three buildings in the centre are to be seen on the left of pictures 108 and 111. Only the facade of the WT offices remains today. (R.M.Casserley)

118.   To confuse any enemy invaders, all nameboards had to be removed. Hence the WT eliminated half of its name. The curious spelling of trolleys was still to be seen in March 1957. (R.M.Casserley)

119.   The GWR operated the Wantage-Swindon service and Thornycroft UV4083 was
photographed on this run at Ashbury. There were extra journeys between Wantage and Wantage
Road station. The route was transferred to the City of Oxford Motor Services in 1932.
(J.M.Cummings coll.)

K 3.   WANTAGE   TRAMWAY.

WANTAGE ROAD
TO
Grove   Bridge.
SECOND 8d. RETURN.

120.   No. 5 is now in the custody of the Great Western Society at the Didcot Railway Centre, where it is seen operating on 4th October 1975. She was never accompanied by a brake van on the WT. She now lives on as a reminder of a remarkable branch, which was a tramway when convenient. (T.Heavyside)

Middleton Press

Easebourne Lane, Midhurst, W Sussex. GU29 9AZ Tel: 01730 813169 Fax: 01730 812601
Email: sales@middletonpress.co.uk www.middletonpress.co.uk
If books are not available from your local transport stockist, order direct post free UK.

BRANCH LINES
Branch Line to Allhallows
Branch Line to Alton
Branch Lines around Ascot
Branch Line to Ashburton
Branch Lines around Bodmin
Branch Line to Bude
Branch Lines around Canterbury
Branch Lines around Chard & Yeovil
Branch Line to Cheddar
Branch Line around Cromer
Branch Line to the Derwent Valley
Branch Lines to East Grinstead
Branch Lines of East London
Branch Lines to Effingham Junction
Branch Lines around Exmouth
Branch Lines to Falmouth, Helston & St. Ives
Branch Line to Fairford
Branch Lines to Felixstow & Aldeburgh
Branch Lines around Gosport
Branch Lines to Hayling
Branch Lines to Henley, Windsor & Marlow
Branch Line to Hawkhurst
Branch Line to Horsham
Branch Lines around Huntingdon
Branch Line to Ilfracombe
Branch Line to Kingsbridge
Branch Line to Kingswear
Branch Line to Lambourn
Branch Lines to Launceston & Princetown
Branch Lines to Longmoor
Branch Line to Looe
Branch Line to Lyme Regis
Branch Line to Lynton
Branch Lines around March
Branch Lines around Midhurst
Branch Line to Minehead
Branch Line to Moretonhampstead
Branch Lines to Newport (IOW)
Branch Lines to Newquay
Branch Lines around North Woolwich
Branch Line to Padstow
Branch Lines to Princes Risborough
Branch Lines to Seaton and Sidmouth
Branch Lines around Sheerness
Branch Line to Shrewsbury
Branch Line to Tenterden
Branch Lines around Tiverton
Branch Lines to Torrington
Branch Lines to Tunbridge Wells
Branch Line to Upwell
Branch Line to Wantage
Branch Lines of West London
Branch Lines of West Wiltshire
Branch Lines around Weymouth
Branch Lines around Wimborne
Branch Lines around Wisbech

NARROW GAUGE
Austrian Narrow Gauge
Branch Line to Lynton
Branch Lines around Portmadoc 1923-46
Branch Lines around Porthmadog 1954-94
Branch Line to Southwold
Douglas to Port Erin
Douglas to Peel
Kent Narrow Gauge
Northern France Narrow Gauge
Romneyrail
Southern France Narrow Gauge
Sussex Narrow Gauge
Surrey Narrow Gauge
Swiss Narrow Gauge
Vivarais Narrow Gauge

SOUTH COAST RAILWAYS
Ashford to Dover
Bournemouth to Weymouth
Brighton to Worthing
Dover to Ramsgate
Eastbourne to Hastings
Portsmouth to Southampton
Ryde to Ventnor
Southampton to Bournemouth

SOUTHERN MAIN LINES
Basingstoke to Salisbury
Crawley to Littlehampton
Dartford to Sittingbourne
East Croydon to Three Bridges
Epsom to Horsham
Exeter to Barnstaple
Exeter to Tavistock
London Bridge to East Croydon
Orpington to Tonbridge
Tonbridge to Hastings
Salisbury to Yeovil
Sittingbourne to Ramsgate
Swanley to Ashford
Tavistock to Plymouth
Three Bridges to Brighton
Victoria to Bromley South
Victoria to East Croydon
Waterloo to Windsor
Waterloo to Woking
Woking to Portsmouth
Woking to Southampton
Yeovil to Exeter

EASTERN MAIN LINES
Barking to Southend
Ely to Kings Lynn
Ely to Norwich
Fenchurch Street to Barking
Hitchin to Peterborough
Ilford to Shenfield
Ipswich to Saxmundham
Liverpool Street to Ilford
Saxmundham to Yarmouth
Tilbury Loop

WESTERN MAIN LINES
Bristol to Taunton
Didcot to Banbury
Didcot to Swindon
Ealing to Slough
Exeter to Newton Abbot
Newton Abbot to Plymouth
Newbury to Westbury
Moreton-in-Marsh to Worcester
Oxford to Moreton-in-Marsh
Paddington to Ealing
Paddington to Princes Risborough
Plymouth to St. Austell
Princes Risborough to Banbury
Reading to Didcot
Slough to Newbury
St. Austell to Penzance
Swindon to Bristol
Taunton to Exeter
Westbury to Taunton

MIDLAND MAIN LINES
St. Albans to Bedford
Euston to Harrow & Wealdstone
Harrow to Watford
St. Pancras to St. Albans

COUNTRY RAILWAY ROUTES
Abergavenny to Merthyr
Andover to Southampton
Bath to Evercreech Junction
Bath Green Park to Bristol
Bournemouth to Evercreech Junction
Brecon to Newport
Burnham to Evercreech Junction
Cheltenham to Andover
Croydon to East Grinstead
Didcot to Winchester
East Kent Light Railway
Frome to Bristol
Guildford to Redhill
Reading to Basingstoke
Reading to Guildford
Redhill to Ashford
Salisbury to Westbury
Stratford upon Avon to Cheltenham
Strood to Paddock Wood
Taunton to Barnstaple
Wenford Bridge to Fowey
Westbury to Bath
Woking to Alton
Yeovil to Dorchester

GREAT RAILWAY ERAS
Ashford from Steam to Eurostar
Clapham Junction 50 years of change
Festiniog in the Fifties
Festiniog in the Sixties
Festiniog 50 years of enterprise
Isle of Wight Lines 50 years of change
Railways to Victory 1944-46
Return to Blaenau 1970-82
SECR Centenary album
Talyllyn 50 years of change
Wareham to Swanage 50 years of change
Yeovil 50 years of change

LONDON SUBURBAN RAILWAYS
Caterham and Tattenham Corner
Charing Cross to Dartford
Clapham Jn. to Beckenham Jn.
Crystal Palace (HL) & Catford Loop
East London Line
Finsbury Park to Alexandra Palace
Holborn Viaduct to Lewisham
Kingston and Hounslow Loops
Lewisham to Dartford
Liverpool Street to Chingford
London Bridge to Addiscombe
Mitcham Junction Lines
North London Line
South London Line
West Croydon to Epsom
West London Line
Willesden Junction to Richmond
Wimbledon to Beckenham
Wimbledon to Epsom

STEAMING THROUGH
Steaming through Cornwall
Steaming through the Isle of Wight
Steaming through Kent
Steaming through West Hants

TRAMWAY CLASSICS
Aldgate & Stepney Tramways
Barnet & Finchley Tramways
Bath Tramways
Brighton's Tramways
Bristol's Tramways
Burton & Ashby Tramways
Camberwell & W.Norwood Tramway
Clapham & Streatham Tramways
Croydon's Tramways
Dover's Tramways
East Ham & West Ham Tramways
Edgware and Willesden Tramways
Eltham & Woolwich Tramways
Embankment & Waterloo Tramways
Exeter & Taunton Tramways
Fulwell - Home to Trams, Trolleys and Buse
Great Yarmouth Tramways
Greenwich & Dartford Tramways
Hammersmith & Hounslow Tramway
Hampstead & Highgate Tramways
Hastings Tramways
Holborn & Finsbury Tramways
Ilford & Barking Tramways
Kingston & Wimbledon Tramways
Lewisham & Catford Tramways
Liverpool Tramways 1. Eastern Rout
Liverpool Tramways 2. Southern Ro
Liverpool Tramways 3. Northern Rou
Maidstone & Chatham Tramways
Margate to Ramsgate
North Kent Tramways
Norwich Tramways
Reading Tramways
Seaton & Eastbourne Tramways
Shepherds Bush & Uxbridge Tramwa
Southend-on-sea Tramways
South London Line Tramways 1903-3
Southwark & Deptford Tramways
Stamford Hill Tramways
Twickenham & Kingston Tramways
Victoria & Lambeth Tramways
Waltham Cross & Edmonton Tramwa
Walthamstow & Leyton Tramways
Wandsworth & Battersea Tramways

TROLLEYBUS CLASSICS
Bradford Trolleybuses
Croydon Trolleybuses
Derby Trolleybuses
Hastings Trolleybuses
Huddersfield Trolleybuses
Maidstone Trolleybuses
Portsmouth Trolleybuses
Reading Trolleybuses

WATERWAY ALBUMS
Kent and East Sussex Waterways
London to Portsmouth Waterway
West Sussex Waterways

MILITARY BOOKS
Battle over Portsmouth
Battle over Sussex 1940
Blitz over Sussex 1941-42
Bombers over Sussex 1943-45
Bognor at War
Military Defence of West Sussex
Military Signals from the South Coas
Secret Sussex Resistance
Surrey Home Guard

OTHER RAILWAY BOOKS
Index to Middleton Press Stations
Industrial Railways of the South-Eas
South Eastern & Chatham Railways
London Chatham & Dover Railway
London Termini - Past and Proposed
War on the Line (SR 1939-45)

96